COMMEMORATIVE STAMP COLLECTION

1994

RUDOLPH
VALENTINO in Rex Beach's A SAINTED DEVIL

CONTENTS

Top: The "last spike" joining East and West railroad tracks was driven as officials and workers watched at Promontory, UT. Second photo: Not one but two heads compete to redirect a soccer ball. Bottom: Charles Chaplin acknowledged as one of the greatest film talents of all time. His "Tramp" character was beloved throughout the world. Bottom left: A Victorian dove from The Gifted Line archival collection in Point Richmond, CA. Facing page: Rudolph Valentino's smoldering sex appeal in **The Sainted Devil**. Inset: a poster advertises Valentino's role as a swashbuckler from the same film.

The Postal Service's 1994 stamp program had something for everyone: anniversaries, sports, space, performing artists, the sea, history, flowers, love, locomotives, a famous labor leader, endangered species, artists, legends, a journalist, an educator, an author/artist, black soldiers, holiday stamps and a puppy to greet the Lunar New Year. They're here. ✑ Anniversaries were important. The fourth in the five-year World War II series marked the 50th year since the allied invasion of Europe on June 6, 1944. The 10 stamps portray action in two theaters of war that led to defeat of the Axis. Edward R. Murrow, noted reporter, brought nightly news about the war from England, and America's popular artist, Norman Rockwell, pictured the Four Freedoms for which we fought on stamps. Murrow and Rockwell also appeared on stamps in 1994. ✑ Five stamps in January previewed the Winter Olympic Games in Lillehammer, Norway, with colors matching the Olympic rings' logo. In May, three stamps welcomed the World Cup championship soccer games, hosted by the United States for the first time. ✑ Dr. Allison Davis, distinguished African American educator and author, appeared on a Black Heritage Series stamp the first year he became eligible. George Meany, the great leader of the AFL-CIO, worked tirelessly to achieve fair pay and good working conditions for all Americans. ✑ Author/artist James Thurber, appearing on a stamp this year and whose work still makes people laugh, was one of the country's most talented humorists. The caricatures of 10 silent screen stars, drawn by the incomparable Al Hirschfeld, captured each actor's persona, leaving no doubt as to his or her identity. ✑ Of the eight Jazz and Blues Singers in the Legends of American Music series, seven were African Americans who brought style and rhythm to this original art form. Also celebrated were five popular singers whose work on radio, stage, screen and television brought instant recognition. ✑ Garden flowers were envelope brighteners, and all five posies can be grown in most parts of the country. ✑ Legends of the West, a 20-

Top: Edward R. Murrow's career as an outstanding broadcast journalist brought him numerous awards. Second photo: A downhill racer at the Lillehammer Winter Olympic Games. Third photo: These women flee their home in Kerkrade, Holland, caught in the line of fire between opposing forces in World War II. Illustration: Famous American artist Frederic Remington made numerous sketches of Buffalo Soldiers in the field. Facing page: A prize-winning rose grown and exhibited in 1993 in Portland, Oregon.

stamp sheetlet, introduces a Classic Collection Series. The western frontier had lawmen, outlaws, miners, settlers, and Native Americans who struggled to preserve their way of life. Although the Buffalo Soldiers stamp is not in this series, their role was important to peacekeeping in the West. ✑ In keeping with historic subjects, antique locomotives appeared in the second of a series on steam engines. The most famous of this issue was the General, captured by saboteurs, then re-captured by Confederate soldiers in the Civil War. ✑ How vital were trains to the nation's growth? Just 125 years ago, on May 10, 1869, east met west at Promontory, Utah, where a golden spike was driven to complete the intercontinental railway system. Could anyone then predict that in July 1969 Americans would rocket to the Moon, land on it, then return safely to Earth? A stamp commemorated the 25th anniversary of the moon landing this July. ✑ Italian Renaissance artist Elisabetta Sirani's *Madonna and Child* is the first painting by a woman to appear on a traditional Holiday stamp. The contemporary Holiday stamp, although modern in appearance, had traditional roots in France where nuns honored Saint Nicholas by giving gifts to the poor. ✑ North America's whooping crane and China's black-necked crane were a joint issue by China and the United States, signifying peace and friendship. Both magnificent birds are endangered, but each country is trying to preserve the species. ✑ Although the Wonders of the Sea stamps appear serene and idyllic, we should be reminded that few locales are left that accommodate scuba divers, and vigilance is needed to protect the oceans' ecological balances and their bounties. ✑

Top: Buffalo Bill Cody's pearl-handled gun. Second photo: The young Nat "King" Cole was as gifted a pianist as he was a vocalist. Third photo: When Clara Bow moved to Paramount Pictures in the 1920s from the small independent Arrow film company, her career soared. She made pictures with names like **Rough House Rosie** *and* **Wild Party** *that promised more naughtiness than they portrayed. Bottom: James Thurber's self-portrait, which became the 1994 commemorative stamp. Facing page: Bing Crosby's voice and relaxed style were often imitated but rarely equaled or topped.*

Place 4-Stamp Souvenir Sheet Here

At age 16, Norman Rockwell had his first commission to illustrate four Christmas cards. From then on, everything was uphill for the artist who called himself a "storyteller," adding, "though this may not be the highest form of art it is what I love to do." ✍ Born in New York City in 1894, he left school as a sophomore to enter art school. At 17 he illustrated his first book, and at 19 he became art director for *Boy's Life* magazine. At a fellow artist's urging, he prepared two cover illustrations and one sketch and personally carried them to the *Saturday Evening Post*'s offices in Philadelphia. He was overjoyed to learn his two covers were accepted, they wanted the sketch completed, and he was commissioned to do three more covers. He was 22. Soon after that he married Irene O'Connor.

✍ Rockwell tried to enlist when the country entered World War I. Rejected for being underweight, he stuffed himself with food, was accepted on the second try, and sent to the Navy Yard in Charleston, South Carolina. When his superiors learned he was an artist, he worked on a Navy publication and achieved celebrity status illustrating visiting "brass." In his free time, he fulfilled contracts for the *Saturday Evening Post, Colliers, Life, Country Gentleman, Literary Digest* and *Popular Science*. From his first *Saturday Evening Post* cover in May 1916 to his last in 1963, he created 321 original cover illustrations. He also had a long association with the Boy Scouts as a poster, calendar and book illustrator, and provided art for numerous other magazines and advertisers. His themes conveyed values and gentle humor with which viewers could identify. If you didn't get the point of his work, he said the art was a failure. ✍ His Navy service over in 1918, he returned to New Rochelle, New York, where he was highly regarded in artistic circles and was already wealthy. He traveled the next few years to Europe, South America and North Africa. He was divorced in 1923. ✍ In 1930, Rockwell married

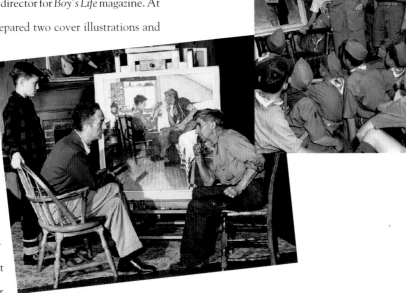

Top: In 1950 Rockwell gave his painting of George Washington to the Boy Scouts organization during their National Jamboree at Valley Forge, PA. Below: Rockwell discusses a calendar painted for the Ford Motor Company's 50th Anniversary with Arlington, VT, home-town models. Facing page: A youthful Rockwell in his studio. Left inset: The **Saturday Evening Post's** *cover on March 9, 1929, showed a family doctor's strategy for building trust in a wary patient. Right inset: A clear victory was worth the trip to the principal's office as shown on the May 23, 1953,* **Saturday Evening Post** *cover.*

Richard D. Sheaff, of Boston, MA, is the designer/ typographer of the Norman Rockwell triple self-portrait stamp. He also designed the Four Freedoms souvenir sheet reproducing Rockwell's art inspired by President Roosevelt's speech to Congress during World War II. Sheaff also designed this year's James Thurber stamp.

Mary Barstow three weeks after they met in Los Angeles. They had three sons, Jerry, Tommy and Peter, and moved to Arlington, Vermont in 1939. ∾ He sought and welcomed suggestions and criticism, and used his neighbors, his sons, towns-people, even himself—in a pinch—as models. He collected old furniture and clothing to create atmosphere. Before illustrating Mark Twain's *Tom Sawyer* and *Adventures of Huckleberry Finn* in 1939, he went to Hannibal, Missouri, to absorb the surroundings. Praising Twain's stories, he said "There was a picture on every page." ∾ In 1943, several paintings and most of his "props," which he had collected for several years to add authenticity to his work, were destroyed when a fire destroyed his Arlington studio. ∾ He was 25 years into his career before he used photography as a tool. Photos relieved models from tedious posing, allowing him to focus on design and details. ∾ He moved to Stockbridge, Massachusetts in 1953. Six years later, his wife died. He married Molly Punderson in 1961. ∾ Two years later his association with the *Saturday Evening Post* ended. His last cover, December 14, 1963, was a portrait of President Kennedy. ∾ In 1941, President Roosevelt asked Congress for Lend-Lease aid for nations fighting the Axis, and made a plea for freedom of speech and freedom of worship, and freedom from want

and freedom from fear. It inspired Rockwell's Four Freedoms art in the *Post* in 1943 and brought millions of requests for reprints. Posters widely circulated by the government raised money for war relief. ∾ Rockwell's coverage of two world wars and American life spanned more than 60

*Top: Rockwell spent hours of concentrated work to produce his art. Center: A photo of the artist provided the basis for Rockwell's February 13, 1960 **Post** cover and the 1994 commemorative stamp. Below: Rockwell stands between the 1972 portraits of Senator and Mrs. McGovern (left) and President and Mrs. Nixon (right) which he painted for the **Ladies Home Journal**.*

years. He received the nation's highest civilian award, the Presidential Medal of Freedom, from President Ford in 1977. He died at Stockbridge, Massachusetts at age 84. Rockwell's art is an imaginary documentary of his time. His scenes caused people to think and to laugh. ∾

Place
Stamp
Here

Place Stamps Here

Whether blooming in a tiny garden or beside a mansion, held in a small, dirt-smudged fist or displayed in a magnificent vase, flowers are an eloquent expression of beauty. They grace ceremonies of all sorts and nourish our souls. ✑ The five garden flowers on 1994 stamps can be grown in most parts of the country by using common sense and patience. Libraries and book stores supply instructions; garden clubs and catalogs offer inspiration and encouragement. If vegetables and weeds can grow in a piece of land, so can these flowers. Proper drainage, six hours of daily sunlight, soil free of competing tree roots and sometimes added nutrients help fill the bill. ✑ Zinnias and marigolds originated in North and Central America. Marigolds were admired by the Aztecs for their beauty and were believed to cure hiccups and help people struck by lightning. Spaniards brought marigolds from Mexico in the 1500s to Spain, France, Africa and India, and they were reintroduced to North America in the late 1700s. ✑ The zinnia grows in every color but blue. A single-stemmed flower, its bloom can be as small as an inch in diameter or as wide as seven inches. It was named for an 18th century botany professor, Johann Gottfried Zinn, but is a true American native plant from the Southwest, Mexico and Central America. ✑ The lily was cultivated centuries ago in the Orient, and people even ate its bulbs. Lilies' colors range from white to pink, yellow, orange and red, and some grow to be five feet tall. Most have an overwhelming fragrance. ✑ The gladiolus, a member of the iris family, originated in Africa. Its Latin name means "small sword." It grows from a corm, unlike the lily, which grows from a bulb. Besides producing a showy flower, the corm grows clusters of pea-sized cormels. After separation from the parent, cormels are then stored and treated to propagate new flowers. ✑ The rose, worth the efforts of a home gardener, differs greatly from its primitive ancestor, a five-petaled plant native to the northern hemisphere's wastelands. After countless mutations, artificial and natural hybridization, many varieties now exist. The rose sends messages of affection, apology, sympathy or joy with equal effect. ✑

Left: These gladioli provide handsome pyramids of blooms. Below: Marigolds grow in a wide range of yellow, red and orange colors. Facing page: The yellow rose is loved in Texas and everywhere else. Left inset: Sturdy hybrids, the "Dreamland" zinnias boast four-inch-wide flowers on 12-inch-high stems. Right inset: Day lilies, ever elegant and lovely, rival the beauty of exotic orchids.

The booklet of five Summer Flowers, designed by National Geographic Society illustrator Ned Seidler of Hampton Bay, NY, is a worthy sequel to his 1993 Spring Flowers booklet. Former Seidler designs were the St. Francis of Assisi and Express Mail stamps and the Montgomery Blair aerogramme.

Top: CBS reporters Murrow (left), Charles Collingwood (center) and Eric Severeid. Right: Murrow donned a war correspondent's uniform when America entered World War II. Facing page: Rarely without a cigarette, Murrow brought a news magazine into the nation's homes with his TV show, **See It Now**. Left inset: Murrow preferred radio to television, and when he left CBS, a parting tribute was his microphone. Right inset: Murrow lights Marilyn Monroe's cigarette preceding her appearance on the April 8, 1955, **Person to Person** show.

Chris Calle, designer of the 1994 George Meany and Dr. Allison Davis stamps, and co-designer with his father, Paul Calle, of this year's Moon Landing stamp, is also responsible for the Edward R. Murrow stamp illustration.

Edward R. Murrow, the most respected and listened-to reporter of his time, is the first broadcast journalist to appear on a U.S. postage stamp. His style was clear and incisive, never pompous or condescending. He believed in the public's right to receive truthful information—both good news and bad—and he tried to explain and evaluate events. ✍ As he broadcasted from building tops during Nazi air raids on London, and flew with Allied bombers in attacks against Germany, his career soared. He did not disguise his rage when reporting the horrors of Buchenwald's death camp. ✍ Murrow was born in Guilford County, North Carolina, on April 25, 1908, and his family moved to Washington state when he was a boy. He majored in speech and broadcasting journalism at Washington State College and graduated with Phi Beta Kappa honors. After college, he arranged foreign student exchange programs in New York. He met Janet Huntington Brewster, and they were married in 1934. ✍ The Columbia Broadcasting System hired Murrow in 1935 to arrange network programs, and he became its director of talks in 1937. Based in London, he was in Europe when Hitler seized Austria in March 1938. He helped coordinate the first live broadcast from five European capitals to America. He said later he "saw Europe tear up its maps, and the full tide of war sweeping across Europe like a brown stain," and he "got to know Britain in her darkest and finest hour." ✍ At the war's end in 1945, he became CBS's vice president for news and public affairs, and he began broadcasting a nightly news program in 1947, which continued for 13 years. He traveled to Korea and, with Fred W. Friendly, produced the first TV documentary on a U.S. war. ✍ In 1953, he and Friendly produced a television program exposing the demagogic tactics of Senator Joseph R. McCarthy, who was later censured by the Senate. ✍ Among his award-winning radio and TV productions were *See It Now*, *Hear It Now* and *Person to Person*. ✍ President Kennedy named him Director of the U.S. Information Agency in 1961. Murrow died in 1965 at his farm in Pawling, New York, survived by his wife Janet and son Casey. ✍

Place
Stamp
Here

Only a proportionally small number of people can enjoy firsthand the exotic colors, shapes and sizes of the sea creatures that inhabit coastal waters. Scuba diving and snorkeling can be a costly adventure. Just getting to where it can be practiced requires transportation, special equipment and skilled, experienced guides who know how this activity can be safely enjoyed. ✑ The four sea stamps issued in 1994 picture divers, fish, mammals and coral from several oceans around the world in totally different environments. They represent the merest fraction of the hundreds of species that inhabit the deep. Divers are limited to areas and temperatures of water they can explore. ✑ The stamps represent an interesting fact: the first life to inhabit our planet developed in the seas. The most advanced form of life—man—emerged and evolved from those beginnings millions of years ago. To sea creatures, marine living is natural; mankind needs artificial means to permit breathing under water. ✑ Still, the most radical changes in man's experiences with the seas have occurred only within the last few centuries of exploration, colonization and population growth. For centuries, because the seas were so vast, it was believed they could accept and dissolve mankind's refuse without costly consequences. Now, despite the fact that the oceans cover 71 percent of the Earth's surface, they no longer offer practicable areas to dispose of man's waste materials. ✑ The Moon, with its extreme temperatures and on which there is no life or water to sustain life, enormously affects the tides—far more than the Sun because it is so much closer to Earth. In turn, the tides affect creatures of the seas and mankind. For example, we know that oysters and mussels depend upon tides to bring food to them they cannot seek for themselves. Areas once famed for the abundance of food fish have experienced serious losses for reasons including overharvesting, agricultural runoffs, damaged estuaries and spawning areas. ✑ The seas dictate our weather conditions. Cycles of warm and cold climates throughout Earth's history have affected man's ability to adapt to them. Scientists can now measure and estimate results of those trends. The current warming cycle, largely brought about by the melting of glaciers and polar regions, is predicted to raise the world's sea levels by four to seven feet by the year 2100—just

Top: Palau is home for this sea turtle. Bottom: Coral reefs in Java waters took eons to grow, and even small breakages harm important biological sites. Facing page: This Fiji Island clownfish swims among poisonous tentacles of a sea anemone without being stung because its slimy skin prevents capture. The clownfish, returning the courtesy, cleans debris from the anemone. Top inset: A crowd of non-stinging jellyfish in tropical waters. Bottom inset: Sea anemones, luring and beautiful, are carnivorous animals, not undersea gardens, and they feed on fish that wander into their grasp.

Charles Lynn Bragg, of Los Angeles, CA, is the son of artists who inspired him to develop his talents. His Wonders of the Sea designs express vast knowledge of his subject combined with reverence for nature's beauty and its vulnerability to man's harmful proclivities.

106 years hence. This not only will affect shoreside residences and recreational areas but it will affect tides, estuaries and spawning grounds. It is as important to apply environmental research and protection for man as it is to benefit the creatures of the sea and their survival. ✍ Overfishing and environmental factors in parts of the world that once supplied plentiful catches of cod, salmon, flounder, tuna, hake and trout, to mention a few, have given ecologists, environmentalists, conservationists and governments great cause for concern, not only for the threat to such valuable food resources but for the livelihood of thousands who rely upon the fishing industry. The issue is being seriously studied in all of the affected areas and it is hoped that for the benefit of all—for this and future generations—that cooperative methods, however costly, will protect and replenish dwindling stocks. ✍ Now, more than ever before, all nations must look to the future. Toxic runoffs, dumping of pollutants, oil spills, damming rivers critical to fish

who swim upstream to spawn, overfishing of some food fish, offshore drilling, which can gravely affect plankton—the basic food of all ocean creatures—these and other damaging practices must be carefully monitored and limited. The continuation of sea life affects everyone—those who make their living providing food from the seas, and those of us who eat it. ✍ The deep oceans are mankind's last frontier on Earth. Scientific explorations are now aided by sophisticated technology. Submersibles probe the abyss, and satellites provide details of subsurface volcanic ranges and trenches and of the dynamic exchanges between the oceans and the Earth's core. ✍ We cannot survive without the oceans. Earth is the only known planet within our galaxy to have this unique condition of land and seas. The notion of colonizing outer space is far less realistic than the conscious effort we can and must make to cherish and protect our seas and the remarkable and life-sustaining creatures within them. ✍

Top: A pair of dolphins in Hawaii's waters. Center: A fluted giant clam from the southwest Pacific. Bottom: A school of banded butterfly fish move through a coral reef in the Red Sea. Facing page: A diver explores Fiji Island coral reefs. Top inset: As the hermit crab grows, it looks for a larger shell to call home. Center inset: The queen angelfish, in the Florida Keys and Caribbean waters. Bottom inset: The Garibaldi lives in southern California waters by rocky shores and kelp beds. Protected by California, it is the state fish.

Place
Stamp
Here

Plains Indians called African American troops on the western front "buffalo soldiers" because their hair reminded them of the buffalo's coat, and the name was a tribute to their courage. The 10th Cavalry placed a buffalo on its regimental crest in the early 1920s. The 9th and 10th Cavalries were the first to be called that name, but it also came to be applied to the 24th and 25th black Infantries. ☙ During the Civil War, black regiments were formed by the North, totaling nearly 185,000 men, some 10 percent of the Union forces. Segregation was the rule. All the officers were white and the enlisted men black. Some officers were unprejudiced, others dictatorial and insensitive. Why did African Americans join the army? Discrimination was more prevalent in civilian life in some parts of the country, and an enlisted man got $13 a month, plus food, clothing and quarters. ☙ In 1867, the 9th and 10th Cavalries began 24 years of continuous service on the Great Plains, along the Rio Grande, in New Mexico, Arizona, Texas, Kansas and the Dakotas. Their mission was clear: to subdue hostile Indians who fiercely resented whites' encroachment on their traditional lands. They protected white settlers and travelers from Indians, robbers, horse thieves and cattle rustlers. They repaired and built post buildings, escorted stagecoaches, built military roads and guarded water holes and railway construction lines. Indians struck and vanished swiftly, seizing horses, food, weapons and clothing for their families in hiding. ☙ The soldiers' clothing and equipment were often inadequate. Bad weather severely tested them on long marches, and illness was a serious problem. ☙ The army hired Indian scouts to locate renegades. They learned the best time to hunt them was in the winter. The Indians often escaped but left food and equipment behind, creating greater hardships and increasing their enmity. By 1880, most of the Indians were forced to move to reservations, and in the late 1880s and early 1900s many western military posts were abandoned. Most of the black troops were reassigned and some served in the Philippines in the Spanish-American War. ☙ Eighteen black enlisted men, including 11 from the 9th Cavalry, received Medals of Honor for heroism in the Indian wars. ☙

Left: A retired Sergeant-Major of the Buffalo Soldiers, wearing full dress uniform and his Medal of Honor, was conceptualized by artist Paul Rossi. Right: The 10th Cavalry's regimental crest.

Facing page: Tenth Cavalry Buffalo Soldiers were subjects of an original painting by Nick Eggenhofer depicting the Battle of Rattlesnake Springs. Top inset: Non-commissioned officers of Troop L, 9th Cavalry, at Fort Wingate, NM, around 1890. Some were possibly Regimental Band members. Bottom inset: A 10th Cavalry escort to General Merritt's party stops for lunch at St. Mary's, MT, in 1894.

Mort Kunstler, one of today's premier Civil War artists, created the Buffalo Soldiers stamp. Brooklyn College, U.C.L.A., the Pratt Institute and work with the National Geographic Society prepared him for one-man shows, TV coverage and books featuring his exciting, accurate work.

Top: A luge competitor at the Winter Olympics. Right: An ice hockey goaltender prepares to defend his goal. Facing page: A competitive racer skis downhill at breakneck speed. Top inset: Strength and endurance are demanded of the cross country ski racers. Bottom inset: Athletic skill and precision, achieved after hours of practice, result in skating pairs' thrilling performances.

Lon Busch, sports enthusiast and advertising art specialist of St. Louis, MO, created an encore for his 1992 Winter Olympic stamps with five stamps celebrating the 1994 Winter Olympic Games in Lillehammer, Norway. His previous designs include the 1991 Basketball stamp.

Stamp concepts, designs and printing have taken a giant leap forward since the United States issued its first Winter Olympic Games stamp at Lake Placid, New York, on January 25, 1932. That stamp, featuring a ski jumper, was prepared and issued in haste, which severely compromised both design and execution. Its only "plus" was the fact that it was the first U.S. Olympic Games stamp. The Summer Games stamp, issued on June 15 that year, redeemed the earlier disappointment with a much better design. ❧ The 1994 Winter Games stamps represent five popular competitive sports. The designs combine the concepts of speed, daring, grace, endurance, athleticism and teamwork, and they also demonstrate the great improvements made in stamp production in the past 62 years. ❧ The first U.S. Olympic Games stamp in 1932 was printed in one color—red. Not until the Overrun Countries series, issued in 1943-1944, would two colors appear on a stamp. ❧ The 1994 Winter Games stamps incorporate the five colors of the Olympic symbol—blue, yellow, black, green and red—which appeared on the newly created Olympic flag at the 1920 Games at Antwerp, Belgium. Eight years later, Portugal included the five interlocking rings on its Olympic stamps, and eventually other nations began the practice; the United States placed the rings on the 1960 Winter Olympic stamp. ❧ At least one of the colors of the rings appears in the flags of the nations competing in the Games. The rings symbolize the five continents at the time of the first modern Olympic Games in 1896. ❧ From the first U.S. Olympic Games stamp in 1932 through the 1994 Winter Games, the grand total of stamps is now 54. This does not include the postal stationery, which has also found popular acceptance. Hundreds of stamps have been issued by other countries participating in the Games throughout the years. ❧ Skiing (including cross-country and jumping) has appeared on seven U.S. stamps. The luge event appears for the first time in 1994. Five different ice skating events have been represented; including 1994's stamp, ice hockey has appeared three times. Beginning in 1972, the five Olympic colors have been creatively included in the stamps' figures, backgrounds or rings. ❧ Sixty-six countries sent competitors to the XVIIth Winter Games held in Lillehammer, Norway. ❧

Place Stamps Here

Place 10-Stamp Sheet Here

I n 1944, Allied forces at opposite sides of the earth faced some of their heaviest battles retaking land seized by the Axis powers. General D. D. Eisenhower was supreme commander in the European sector, and General Douglas MacArthur in the southwest Pacific. ✍ In Italy, Germans resisted Allied attacks through the severe winter of 1943-1944. In May the Germans began to withdraw, and Rome was liberated on June 4. Total victory was not won until 1945. ✍ On June 6, 1944, the largest invasion force ever as-sembled, composed of American, British and Canadian units, crossed the English Channel and landed on a 60-mile-long front of the Normandy coast. Called *Operation Overlord*, its aim was to free Europe from Nazi domina-tion. ✍ Allied planes towing gliders and carrying paratroopers led the assault. The invasion caught the Germans off guard, they failed to counterattack immediately, and confusion and tactical errors temporarily put them at a severe disadvantage. Before D-Day, German Field Marshal Erwin Rommel had predicted: "If we can't throw the enemy into the sea within 24 hours, then that will be the beginning of the end." Less than one year later, Hitler would commit suicide on April 30, Berlin would fall on May 2, and Germany would surrender on May 7, 1945. ✍ Despite heavy casualties during the invasion, the Allies secured a foothold on the beaches. To complicate matters, on June 19 a hurricane struck the area, cutting supplies to a trickle for four days. The capture of Cherbourg on June 27 was a decisive gain. The port, as other strategic landing areas, had to be cleared of mines, a perilous task for minesweepers and divers. Meanwhile, German land defenses bottled up the Allies before their successful breakout beginning July 25. ✍ By July 2, a million troops, a half million tons of supplies and some 171,000 vehicles had been landed. Total losses of the Normandy campaign alone were an estimated 637,000, including prisoners of war. Americans lost 20,838 killed and 94,881 wounded. Some 200,000 Germans were killed and

Left: Members of Company E, 502nd Paratroopers, are given the "full victory, nothing else" message by Commander-in-Chief "Ike" Eisenhower before they board planes to participate in D-Day's first assault on June 6, 1944. Below: Wounded assault troops of the 16th Infantry Regiment await evacuation from Omaha Beach to field hospitals. Facing page: Clutching a few possessions, a woman in Siegburg, Germany, flees from a burning building.

Bill Bond, of Arlington, VA, a National Geographic Society artist, put his own and the Allies' war experiences on record with his fourth of five miniature commemorative sheets that chronicle World War II's history.

Top: In bitter cold during the Battle of the Bulge, Yanks lined up for chow, which meant K-rations, not steak! Second photo: A diving officer and two crewmen of the submarine U.S.S. Batfish prepare to dive. Third photo: A Marine on Saipan carries a scaling rope to climb to the island's highest point, where Japanese troops were dug in. Facing page: B-17 bombers of the Fifteenth Air Force drop a string of bombs on oil storage yards at Regensburg, Germany. Top inset: By the spring of 1944, Flying Fortresses were rarely challenged as most of Germany's planes were destroyed. Second inset: The Red Ball Express, carrying fuel and other priority supplies, had the right-of-way over all vehicles except ambulances. Third inset: The French Tricolor was unfurled at the City Hall of Aix in southern France when the Allied Seventh Army liberated the city. Bottom inset: General MacArthur kept his promise to return to the Philippines and waded ashore during landings on Leyte Island on October 20, 1944.

wounded, and 200,000 more were captured. ‿ As the Allies advanced, the Red Ball Express maintained a continuous supply of essential materials by trucks through France to the fighting forces. Russians praised the system as an astounding feat. Adding fuel containers to American fighter planes enabled them to escort heavy bombers on longer missions. In late February 1944, Allied planes had downed 450 German planes from which the *Luftwaffe* never recovered for lack of trained pilots. ‿ Paris was liberated on August 24. Hitler demanded the city's destruction, but was not obeyed. In late fall, General Eisenhower said that throughout the front, from Switzerland to the mouth of the Rhine, there was "the dirtiest kind of infantry slugging." ‿ In December, German forces mounted Hitler's last major offensive—the Battle of the Bulge in the Ardennes area—against his generals' advice. German *panzers* penetrated Allied defenses on a 70-mile front and surrounded Bastogne. The Germans demanded surrender, the reply was "nuts!" and the besieged forces were saved by a succession of sharp counterattacks. The desperate *blitzkrieg* saw the Germans losing 120,000 dead, captured and wounded besides artillery pieces and tanks they could not afford to lose. ‿ In the vast Pacific sector, the Allies' buildup of men, ships and supplies began taking a toll on the Japanese. New Guinea, seized by Japan in 1942, fell after two years of miserable jungle warfare. U.S. submarines sank more Japanese tonnage than all other naval and air forces combined. By the end of 1944, Japan had 4,000 planes compared with America's 10,000 war planes and 8,000 transports. ‿ In June, Saipan was retaken from Japan after a great loss of life on both sides. In the carrier battle called the Great Marianas Turkey Shoot, Japan lost 500 planes—the U.S. lost 130. ‿ October's Battle of Leyte Gulf began the liberation of the Philippines with huge losses of Japanese warships and men. At year's end, Japan was open to attack from all sides. ‿

If the proof of a pudding is in the eating, the proof of James Thurber's humor is in the reading. His comic genius as an author and cartoonist is as hilarious today as it was 50 years ago. ❧ Born in Columbus, Ohio, on December 8, 1894, Thurber began his career slowly and inauspiciously, but it grew to greatness when he was discovered and published by *The New Yorker* magazine. He had attended Ohio State University from 1913 to 1918. Without graduating, he then became a code clerk for the State Department, where his remarkable memory was as valuable as when he composed essays about his youth, uncommon events and dogs he admired. ❧ Thurber then reported for the *Columbus Dispatch* before he married and went to Europe. He worked two years for the *Chicago Tribune* in Paris and Nice and returned to New York as a reporter for the *Evening Post.* ❧ Almost by accident in 1927, he learned that an emerging magazine, *The New Yorker*, was hiring, and he promptly applied. A failure as an administrator and editor, he was reassigned to writing tasks and shared a small office with the brilliant essayist, E. B. White, five years Thurber's junior. ❧ Both were blessed with a keen comic sense. They had similar backgrounds, having edited college papers at Ohio State and Cornell, respectively. Thurber was ebullient and extroverted; White was reserved. Thurber learned writing disciplines from White and felt deeply indebted to him because "he made me realize a writer turns on his mind, not a faucet." ❧ Thurber's gift for drawing first appeared in a book they coauthored in 1929, *Is Sex Necessary?*—again thanks to White's encouragement. Thurber's cartoons made their debut in *The New Yorker* in 1931, featuring menacing women, bewildered and threatened men, and large dogs with long ears and sad eyes. ❧ Thurber left *The New Yorker* as a staff member in 1933 but continued to be a regular contributor of articles and drawings. By 1940, failing eyesight limited his drawing, and by 1952 he was nearly blind. ❧ James Thurber's legacy includes 17 books, two others with coauthors, and one published posthumously. Twice married, Thurber was the father of a daughter, Rosemary. He died on November 2, 1961, in New York City. ❧

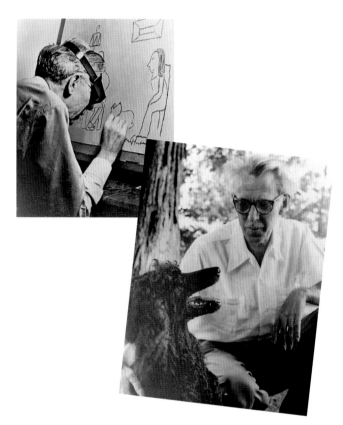

Top: Nearly blind in his late years, Thurber used a loupe to magnify his drawings. Bottom: The humorist/artist and his wife were partial to poodles. Lower left: A Thurber sketch. Facing page: The young Thurber was a voracious reader, and his writing improved under colleague E.B. White's guidance. Left inset: Thurber composed his work by hand and later dictated as his sight failed. Right inset: Peggy Cass, Thurber and Joan Anderson appeared in a skit in "The Thurber Carnival" on Broadway.

Designer/typographer Richard D. Sheaff, of Boston, MA, designed the James Thurber stamp featuring the author/artist's self portrait. Sheaff also designed the Norman Rockwell stamp and souvenir sheet.

Top left: A player dribbles toward the opponents' goal. Top right: Collisions are inevitable when opponents fight to control the ball. Bottom: Teammates cheer their victory. Facing page: Opposing players leap to head a ball toward their teammates.

C. Michael Dudash, designer of the World Cup Soccer stamps, also illustrated last year's popular 1993 Sports Horses. Born in Mankato, MN, the former McGraw-Hill illustrator now does freelance work at his Moreton, VT, studio.

Add them up: the World Series, Wimbledon, the Super Bowl, the College Bowl games, the Stanley Cup, the NBA finals, and for good measure, The Masters in Augusta. Total television viewer estimates are awesome. Beside World Cup Soccer's global audience of two billion fans, the numbers aren't close. Soccer was king as the U.S. hosted World Cup Soccer for one month in 1994. ✑ Soccer, called "football" by every nation except the United States, has so captivated players and spectators that it has spread to undeveloped nations as well as the world's most industrialized countries. Soccer is the second most popular youth sport in the United States. Why? Because it is fun and is a sport that does not require large or tall athletes, just boys, girls, men and women. Small players compete fairly with big ones in their age groups. It is a game calling for total concentration, stamina, strategy, agility, grace, skill, judgment, courage and timing. Youngsters start developing dribbling, passing, shooting and trapping skills with just a soccer ball, some room to practice and some guidance on how to develop those techniques. ✑ The dictionary defines soccer as a game played with a round ball by two teams of 11 players on a field with a goal at either end; the ball is moved chiefly by kicking or by using any part of the body except the hands and arms. Sound simple? Anything but. It is exciting competition, and players the world over have elevated it to the ultimate team sport. ✑ The Postal Service issued three stamps portraying some of the skills repeatedly seen in soccer games. The 29-cent First-Class domestic mail stamp shows a player volleying a ball in the direction of the viewer. Balance and ball control are critical in achieving a pass to a teammate. ✑ The 40-cent stamp, the United States's current international post card rate, shows a player "trapping" the ball high in the air, using his left foot to control its direction. ✑ The 50-cent International First-Class stamp shows a player "heading" or redirecting the ball by keeping his neck stiff and striking the ball just under his hairline. ✑ The three denominations served both domestic and international mailing needs. A souvenir sheet with all three stamps was sold at face value especially for collectors. ✑

Place
40¢
Stamp
Here

Place
50¢
Stamp
Here

Place
29¢
Stamp
Here

The unifying qualities that brought stardom to these five entertainers were their inimitable, individual styles, ability to perform in several mediums, willingness to struggle for recognition and, once it was received, to deliver what people wanted them to do. They loved their work, and it showed. They loved their audiences, and that, too, showed. Through their recordings, films and television shows, we can rediscover their great artistry and be entertained as they would wish. ⌒ Al Jolson (1886-1950) emigrated from Lithuania with his parents in 1894 and was brought up in Washington, D.C. His father, a cantor, wanted Al to succeed him, but Al ran away at 11 to join a show and a circus before returning home. By 1900, he turned professional and performed in vaudeville, burlesque and minstrel shows. He signed with the Shubert brothers in 1911 and won instant acclaim at the Winter Garden. He introduced a blackface character named "Gus" whom he portrayed for most of his stage career. The Shuberts built a ramp leading from the stage to the theater's orchestra seats so Jolson could sing more directly to his audience. He made screen history in 1927 in the first talkie, *The Jazz Singer*, and in 1946 his voice was dubbed in a popular film biography, *The Jolson Story*. He later appeared on radio and TV. ⌒ Bing Crosby (1904-1977), born in Tacoma, Washington, left Gonzaga College before graduating to sing with Paul Whiteman's dance band in 1926. His talent led to his own radio show in 1931 and *Where the blue of the night...* became his theme song. His acting career began in the 1930s when he made several short films for Mack Sennett. *The Big Broadcast* was his first feature film, and it became a stepping stone to many other movies, chiefly musicals, including the *Road* pictures with costars Bob Hope and Dorothy Lamour. He won an Oscar in 1944 for his role in *Going My Way* and also starred in dramatic roles, most notably in *Little Boy Lost*, *The Country Girl* and *Stagecoach*. He was first married to Dixie Lee, who died in 1952, then to Kathryn Grant in 1957. A heart attack after a golf game ended his life in Madrid, Spain. ⌒ Ethel Waters (1896-1977), born in Chester, Pennsylvania, began singing at

Top: Bing Crosby made over 70 movies, and at the time of his death his record sales topped 300 million. In the movies **Going My Way** *and* **The Bells of St. Mary's** *Crosby played a young priest.*
Left: Crosby and Dinah Shore made records and performed on both radio and television together.
Facing page: Al Jolson developed a style that seemed pure ham, but showmanship made it work.
Inset: Jolson's voice improved in later years, and he never failed to earn numerous encores, which he gave generously.

Chris Payne, illustrator of the Popular Singers stamps, received a Fine Arts degree at Miami University in Oxford, OH, and has since taught there. His work has earned him several prestigious awards and appears in numerous major publications. He and his wife, Paula, and their two sons live in Cincinnati.

age 5. She appeared in vaudeville in Philadelphia and Washington before singing in New York in 1917. In the 1920s she was a popular recording star accompanied by top jazzmen and achieved stardom in night clubs and on stage. Ethel had her own show from 1935-1939 and performed at Carnegie Hall in 1938. One of her most unforgettable songs was *Stormy Weather*, which she introduced to her repertoire at the Cotton Club in 1933. Her remarkable dramatic ability to interpret and project each song influenced many singers. Stage and film successes, such as *Cabin in the Sky*, *Mamba's Daughters* and *Member of the Wedding* eventually eclipsed her singing career, and from 1960 to 1975 she toured with evangelist Reverend Billy Graham. ∽ Nat "King" Cole (1919-1965) moved from Alabama to Chicago when he was four, and played the organ and sang in his father's church choir at 12. Nat made his recording debut in 1936 and, strongly influenced by Earl "Fatha" Hines, played with several groups before forming the King Cole Trio. His best jazz recordings dated from the 1940s, and in 1943, his voice solo with the Trio, "Straighten Up and Fly Right" was an instant hit. By the late 1940s he was featured as a vocalist, not a pianist, recording mainly with big bands. He was the first black jazz artist to have his own weekly radio show in 1948-49, and had a weekly television show in 1956-57 as a soloist. He appeared in several movies including a short entitled *The Nat "King" Cole Musical Story* in 1955 and *St. Louis Blues* in 1958, portraying W.C. Handy. ∽ Ethel Merman (1909-1984) was a secretary and worked in vaudeville and cabarets before making her Broadway debut in 1930 in *Girl Crazy*. Despite a lack of musical training, it was said "she was never better than when she strode downstage, planted both feet, reared back and blasted the back wall of the balcony." Brassy and confident, her stage presence brought her top roles. One of her greatest hits was *Call Me Madam*, a parody on Washington hostess Ambassador Perle Mesta, written for her by Irving Berlin. In the musical, *Annie Get Your Gun*, also written by Berlin, Merman wanted to sing "There's No Business Like Show Business." Rogers and Hammerstein worked it into her role, and it became identified with her. She made several films between 1930 and 1954, but they were not as successful as her live performances. ∽

*Top: Ethel Merman projected enthusiasm and personality on radio, stage and television. Bottom left: This portrait of Merman as Annie Oakley in **Annie Get Your Gun** was painted by Rosemarie Sloat. Merman gave it to the Smithsonian's National Portrait Gallery in 1971. Bottom right: Ethel Waters used her flair for dramatics to express intensity and joy in her singing and stage careers. Facing page: Nat "King" Cole's song **"Unforgettable"** was a hit both in his lifetime and after his death. Inset: Cole's talent ranks him among the great jazz pianists.*

Place
Stamp
Here

D r. Allison Davis, eminent psychologist, educator and author, and the first man, black or white, from the field of education to be chosen a fellow of the American Academy of Arts and Sciences, is the 17th person honored in the Black History Series of stamps. ✑ Dr. Davis was a faculty member of the University of Chicago for nearly 40 years. With the cooperation of other research educators, he attacked intelligence testing of students as being culturally biased because the tests did not accurately measure the learning potential of children from low-income families. In a lecture at Harvard University, he said, "We need to start with simple situations, drawn from the early life of the pupil....The situations must also be chosen from the common life of all the pupils so the problems will motivate all social classes....They must be at the molecular level of analysis, so that the child may carry a problem through all the detailed steps to the solution." ✑ Dr. Davis was born in Washington, D.C., in 1902. He received his B.A. degree from Williams College in 1924, his M.A. in English from Howard University in 1925 and an M.A. in anthropology from Howard in 1932. He then studied anthropology at the London School of Economics in 1933. Before joining the University of Chicago faculty, he was associate director of field research in social anthropology at Howard, professor of anthropology at Dillard University in New Orleans, and research associate in psychology at Yale's Institute for Human Relations. He became a research associate at the University of Chicago's Center on Child Development in 1939 and assistant professor in its Education Department in 1942, the same year he received his doctorate. ✑ In 1947, he and another faculty member were the first African Americans granted tenure, and he was named a full professor in 1948. He was named the John Dewey Distinguished Service Professor at Chicago and also taught at Columbia, Michigan and Illinois Universities and at the University of California at Berkeley. ✑ Dr. Davis was a member of the President's Commission on Civil Rights in 1966-67, and he was vice chairman of the Labor Department's Commission on Manpower Training from 1968 to 1972. ✑ Upon his death in 1983 in Chicago, he was survived by his wife, the former Lois Mason, and two sons, Gordon and Allison. ✑

Top: Dr. Allison Davis received his doctorate at the University of Chicago in 1942. Shown are his son, Allison, held by Elizabeth Stubbs Davis; Dr. Davis, and his wife's brother, Dr. Frederick Douglass Stubbs. Bottom: Dr. Davis takes neighborhood youngsters to play baseball in 1949 in Chicago. Facing page: Dr. Davis was photographed at his University of Chicago office in 1968 by his son, Allison. Inset: A workbook exercise in problem-solving prepared by Davis and his colleague, Kenneth Eells, presents a "level playing field" for children of dissimilar backgrounds.

The portrait of distinguished educator and author Dr. Allison Davis is the fourth design in 1994 to carry artist Chris Calle's credits. The George Meany, Edward R. Murrow, and Moon Landing stamps—the latter with the cooperation of his father, veteran stamp designer Paul Calle— are the other three.

Top: Edwin Aldrin was photographed beside a device equipped to detect "solar wind" and return the data to Earth. Below: Neil Armstrong (left), Michael Collins (center) and Edwin Aldrin greet the world from the quarantine trailer on the carrier **Hornet**. Facing page: Edwin Aldrin was photographed with the lunar module and his photographer, Armstrong, reflected on his bubble helmet. The helmets were protected by double visors coated with gold to block the Sun's intense glare, heat and ultraviolet radiation. Inset: Aldrin stands beside the United States flag, treated to stay unfurled because of the lack of wind on the Moon.

Veteran designer Paul Calle, of Stamford, CT, who created the First Man on the Moon stamp 25 years ago, designed the Moon Landing stamp in cooperation with his son, Chris Calle of Ridgefield, CT.

Four days and six hours after *Saturn V*, the world's most powerful multi-stage rocket, boosting moon-bound rocket *Apollo 11*, roared into the sky from Cape Kennedy, Florida, on July 16, 1969, Apollo's smallest component, the four-legged lunar module *Eagle*, carrying astronauts Neil Armstrong and Edwin Aldrin, landed gently on the Moon. ✑ Astronaut Michael Collins, in the command module *Columbia* orbited the Moon 70 miles above them. After *Eagle* landed, Armstrong and Aldrin walked on the Moon, deployed scientific instruments, collected moon samples and described their experiences to the earth 218,096 miles away. ✑ At any stage the trip might have been thwarted and three men's lives lost. Instead, President Kennedy's May 1961 challenge was met that "the United States should commit itself to achieving the goal before this decade is out of landing a man on the moon and returning him safely to earth." Five months and 11 days before the sixties ended, two Americans walked on the Moon, and returned. Millions of hours of construction, experiments, computer set-ups and preparation made the mission possible. The mystical silver Moon was no longer a stranger but a link to future space travel. ✑ Armstrong was in charge, one of the nation's finest pilots; Aldrin was also a pilot and a computer whiz; Collins piloted the command module *Columbia* around the Moon, and prepared to dock with *Eagle's* "ascent half" after it left the Moon. ✑ The Moon's gravity, at 1/6th of Earth's, said Armstrong, was "easier than simulation," as he hopped about his tasks. Aldrin described the Moon's "magnificent isolation" and thanked all those who put them there. After they deployed scientific instruments and placed the flag, President Nixon called them from Earth to praise their achievement. ✑ The two "lunanauts" said the Moon was friendly and hospitable. After two hours' work, they boarded *Eagle*, removed their bulky suits and tried in vain to sleep. They fired *Eagle's* ascent engine, docked with *Columbia*, stored the moon samples and finally slept. After 60 hours of earthward flight, *Columbia's* crew splashed into the Pacific on July 24, was picked up by the carrier *Hornet*, and returned to tumultuous welcomes. A special commemorative sheet of 12 stamps marks their 25th anniversary. ✑

Place
Stamp
Here

Place 20-Stamp Sheet Here

n 1805 the Louisiana Purchase doubled the original 13 states' area and brought adventurous tales of men, women and the land. ∽ HOME ON THE RANGE. Mexican *vaqueros*, the early cowboys who "broke" mustangs and rounded up longhorns, were joined by ex-soldiers and Blacks who drove cattle over many hellish trails for sale in the northern markets. ∽ BUFFALO BILL (1846-1917). William Cody, Pony Express rider, cavalry scout, Indian fighter and buffalo hunter, formed a Wild West Show that toured the U.S. and Europe for 30 years. ∽ JIM BRIDGER (1804-1881) was a guide who founded Fort Bridger, Wyoming, a waystop for the Pony Express, pioneers and the military. He was a master of Indian sign language. ∽ ANNIE OAKLEY (1860-1926) at age 12 helped support her family by shooting and selling game birds. At 15 she outshot marksman Frank Butler, then married him. Their act in Buffalo Bill's show brought them worldwide fame. ∽ NATIVE AMERI-CAN CULTURE, known for its reverence for the environment, its customs and its highly developed art, existed for centuries before explorers displaced tribes and changed the Indians' former way of life. ∽ CHIEF JOSEPH (c.1840-1904), leader of the Oregon Nez Percé tribe, whose ancestral lands were not properly ceded, won admiration for his courageous resistance before surrendering. His tribe was sent to a reservation in Idaho. ∽ BILL PICKETT (1870-1932), the south Texas cowhand who developed "bulldogging," was a range rider whose skills brought him international acclaim. He was the first black enshrined in the National Rodeo Hall of Fame. ∽ BAT MASTERSON (1853-1921), a Dodge City lawman who tracked and brought to justice frontier desperados, parlayed his interest in boxing and racing to became a New York reporter and editor. ∽ JOHN FRÉMONT (1813-1890), whose explorations beyond the Rockies aided western migrations, received national recognition, a court martial, election to the California Senate, military reinstate-ment and nomination for the presidency. ∽ WYATT EARP (1848-1929) had many careers as a lawman, buffalo hunter, gambler, horse thief and saloon keeper. Earp and his three brothers won fame for the gunfight at Tombstone's O.K. Corral. Wyatt was unharmed. ∽ NELLIE CASHMAN (c.1849-1925),

Top: The young Nellie Cashman looks more like a homebody than a miner in this early portrait.
Center: Wild Bill Hickock's derringer probably saw less use than his six-shooter. Below: Bill Pickett's well-used spurs.
Facing page: Buffalo Bill Cody dressed for his Wild West Show, captured many admirers especially in Europe.

The 20-stamp sheetlet, Legends of the West, was illustrated by Mark Hess, of Katonah, NY, whose 1989 Classic Mail Transportation stamps were voted most popular in a national collectors' poll. A successful publication illustrator, his work has appeared on numerous TIME magazine covers.

Top: The real Annie Oakley's costume was similar to Ethel Merman's in the Broadway show **Annie Get Your Gun**. *Center: Indian artistry was vividly expressed on these beaded moccasins.*

Below: This Indian war bonnet with beaded headband and eagle feathers signified its wearer was a Chief.

Facing page: Shoshone guide, Sacagawea guided Lewis and Clark's expedition with her papoose strapped to her back. Top left: Lawman, Bat Masterson was also a fancy dresser. Bottom left: Explorer, John Frémont was popularly called The Pathfinder. Bottom center: The elusive Apache warrior, Geronimo. Bottom right: Lawman, Bill Tilghman "wore many hats" in his colorful lifetime. Top right: Lawman, Wyatt Earp, hero of movies and television.

an Irish girl, was called "Saint of the Sourdoughs" for helping downtrodden miners. She filed gold claims in the West and Alaska, and drove a dog team 750 miles on her way to Tombstone five years before she died. ✍ CHARLES GOODNIGHT (1836-1929), Texas Ranger and leading cattle baron, found routes to drive cattle to northern markets. At Palo Duro Canyon near Amarillo, he improved stock and protected a dwindling bison herd. ✍ GERONIMO (1823-1909) was a Chiricahua Apache leader who fought to preserve the Indians' way of life. He eluded several thousand Mexican and American forces before he was held captive in Florida and retired in Oklahoma. ✍ KIT CARSON (1809-1868), mountain man, trapper, buffalo hunter and guide, joined John Frémont's explorations, fought in the Mexican War, helped quell Indian revolts and sought treaties for Indians. ✍ WILD BILL HICKOCK (1837-1876), a Union scout and spy in the Civil War, earned a reputation as a tough lawman and was a target for gunslingers. While prospecting in Dakota Territory, he was shot in a saloon during a poker game. ✍ WESTERN WILDLIFE suffered immense losses as trappers, settlers and railroad builders took their toll. Buffalo were slain for a cent a pound, and hides sold for a dollar each. Some herds are now being restored. ✍ JIM BECKWOURTH (c.1798-1866), son of black and white Virginian parents, moved west and became a trapper, horse trader and army scout. He joined the Crow tribe, rode in war parties and found a pass through the Rockies now named for him. ✍ BILL TILGHMAN (1854-1924), a crack shot and buffalo and bounty hunter, became a lawman with Bat Masterson, who said he was "the greatest of us all." As deputy U.S. marshal he fought outlaws and became a state senator and police chief. ✍ SACAGAWEA (c.1787-1812), a Shoshone Indian girl, was captured and enslaved by another tribe and later sold to a French trapper. They married, and were hired to guide and interpret for Lewis and Clark's expedition to the Pacific. She is honored by numerous statues. ✍ OVERLAND MAIL was a 25-day coach trip from Memphis and St. Louis to California. Starting in April 1860, Pony Express riders carried mail west in just under 10 days. They were replaced in 18 months by telegraph service. ✍

Since the first Love stamp was issued in 1973, the popularity of its theme has steadily grown, making these stamps an annual favorite. This year's dual issues, with a combination of hearts, flowers and lovebirds, admirably met mailers' expectations. ✍ They also provided an added advantage: namely, a Love stamp meeting postage requirements for letters weighing more than one ounce, or mail that exceeds size limits and calls for a surcharge. ✍ The 29-cent Love stamp, showing a lovebird sitting comfortably on a heart-shaped nest of red roses, carries an intended message beautifully on most First-Class mail. ✍ The 52-cent Love stamp, picturing a colorful basket of roses and two lovebirds, serves mailers sending outsize letters or letters or cards weighing more than one ounce. This is of special benefit for wedding invitations, which are traditionally printed on heavier paper than usual and include acceptance notes for the recipients' convenience. The 52-cent stamp is distinctive on the outer envelope, and the enclosed reply envelope, with the 29-cent Love stamp, perpetuates the theme. By pairing these stamps, mailing costs are made more economical and serve the sender's wish for a singular expression. ✍ Love stamps, issued before Valentine's Day, serve many other occasions as well. Not long after February 14th has passed, other special events when friends exchange greetings follow in rapid succession. St. Patrick's Day comes first, then Passover and Easter, followed by Mother's Day on the second Sunday in May. Then come First Communions, Bar Mitzvahs, Bat Mitzvahs, wedding invitations, Father's Day, birthdays, Grandparent's Day, Rosh Hashanah, Yom Kippur and other occasions. ✍ And what is more welcome to a student or serviceman or servicewoman away from home than letters from one's family or sweetheart? Maybe a check, or snapshot, enclosed? ✍ For the many sizes and varieties of messages now offered by greeting card companies, the Love stamps offer appropriate adornment. Although the 52-cent stamp for overseas mail costs just two cents more than First-Class postage, it can improve international friendship with correspondents abroad. ✍ Since "love makes the world go 'round," the Love stamps are appropriate ambassadors that bring pleasure to recipients young and old alike. ✍

L O V E

Top: Many wedding, anniversary and Valentine's Day messages during the Victorian period were three dimensional, embossed cards such as this flower cart that unfolded to reveal a loving message inside. Bottom: This "basket of love" is very similar to the 1994 Love stamp. Facing page: A romantic picture postcard developed by the Winsch Publishing Co. of the United States was printed in Germany around 1915 during World War I. The Dove Messenger, inset, was typical of Valentines and other greeting cards.

Lon Busch of St. Louis designed the 1994 Love stamps. He was also selected to design the 1994 Winter Olympic Games stamps.

G E O R G E M E A N Y

W A S H I N G T O N D C • A U G U S T 1 6

Top: George Meany, contemplates strategies to accomplish union objectives. Bottom: During a meeting recess, Meany plans the merger of two competitive and dissimilar labor organizations. A unanimous vote united the CIO, and the AFL, ending a 20-year cleavage. Facing page: Meany's concerns were economic dignity, improved working conditions, voting and civil rights for working men and women and a halt to union corruption. Inset: AFL-CIO's president Meany addresses a union meeting. In Meany's long tenure, he dealt with eight U.S. presidents and some frequently consulted him.

The George Meany stamp was designed by Chris Calle, of Ridgefield, CT. Calle designed last year's se-tenant Deaf Communication stamps and the Dean Acheson stamp.

George Meany, one of the most influential American labor leaders of the 20th century, whose career covered six decades, became a spokesman for the working man. As president of the 14-million-member American Federation of Labor and the Congress of Industrial Organizations (AFL-CIO), he said in 1967, "The results of collective bargaining have brought—over time—the most profound and revolutionary changes and improvements in the pattern of our national and family life." He was an instrument of that process. Born in New York City in 1894, he followed his father in the plumbing trade at age 16. He dropped out of high school and enrolled in trade school. After apprenticeship, he was accepted into the plumbers' union and plied his trade until 1922. He then became a business agent, supplying union members for building trade jobs. His honesty and sensitivity to the needs of labor eventually led to increasingly responsible positions. When he was 22, Meany's father and older brother died, and George became sole support of his mother, six siblings and a maternal grandparent. He met Eugenia McMahon and courted and married her, and they subsequently had three daughters. Putting the jobless to work, he told unions, business, the Congress and eight U.S. presidents, "would control inflation and boost the economy." He played a key role in rallying the work force to top levels of production during World War II. Meany was intolerant of being lied to, shoddy workmanship on a job, corruption within unions and Communism. If someone lied to him, that ended the relationship; if workmanship was poor, he said "tear it out." He believed in using all lawful means to improve working conditions: strikes, boycotts and legislative lobbying. His causes were unemployment insurance, voting rights, minimum wages, human rights, equal opportunity and fair labor legislation. He was one of the first to advocate national health insurance. After being secretary-treasurer of the AFL for 13 years, he was chosen president and brought about the merger of the AFL with the CIO. His interests went beyond the domestic scene, and he was influential in international trade unionism. He died in 1980.

Place
Stamp
Here

Place Stamps Here

efore radio, silent movies had no competition for mass entertainment audiences, and the stars of the twenties wielded enormous influence. Their clothing, hair styles, language and behavior were copied by fans. The lack of sound did not limit them. Their films, preserved in archives and TV documentaries, reveal the creative talents that led to the art form we enjoy today. ✒ RUDOLPH VALENTINO (1895-1926), born in Italy, was a taxi dancer in New York before he found work dancing in musicals and bit parts in films. His dark, good looks led to his discovery in *The Four Horsemen of the Apocalypse*, and his role in *The Sheik* catapulted him to stardom. He died in New York at age 31 and was mourned as the great male sex symbol of silent films. ✒ CLARA BOW (1905-1965) was called the "It" girl and was an icon of the Jazz Age. Born into a poor family in Brooklyn, she won a beauty contest, went to Hollywood and appeared in 14 films. Her "flapper" manner appealed to both men and women, and she performed with many leading male stars. She succeeded in the "talkies," but public scandals turned audiences against her. Before her death she bequeathed her sex symbol "crown" to Marilyn Monroe. ✒ SIR CHARLES CHAPLIN (1889-1977), knighted in England in 1975, spent two boyhood years in an orphanage and often lived on the street. A son of music-hall performers, by age 8 he toured with a troupe. At 17 he came to America and acted in 35 comedies for Mack Sennett. As "The Tramp" he was famous worldwide but his politics created ill will and he moved to Switzerland. He received an Oscar at the 1972 Academy Awards Ceremony. ✒ LON CHANEY (1883-1930) used pantomime to communicate with his deaf parents. A vaudeville veteran, he went to Hollywood in 1914, mastered makeup art, and earned fame making macabre films. *The Hunchback of Notre Dame* and *The Phantom of the Opera* aroused both pity and revulsion. He made one "talkie" in 1930 and died that same year. ✒ JOHN GILBERT (1897-1936), a son of theatrical parents, began in films in 1916 and didn't achieve stardom until 1925. Gossip fed rumors of a love affair with Greta Garbo, and their passionate love scenes on film added fuel to the flame. Many

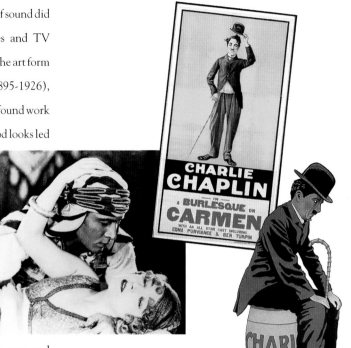

Top: A Chaplin "Tramp" poster. The 1915 film was considered his first masterpiece.
Bottom left: Women swooned over Valentino's love-making scenes in **The Sheik**. *Bottom right: Artist Roberty, of France, titled his 1917 Chaplin Poster "Charlot."*
Facing page: The dimpled Clara Bow in an appealing pose. She is regarded as Hollywood's first true sex symbol. Top inset: Lon Chaney, the "man of a thousand faces" without makeup. Below: Chaney as Quasimodo, in **The Hunchback of Notre Dame**. *He is known as one of the world's great character actors.*

Al Hirschfeld of New York City, who has been a premier celebrity caricaturist for more than half a century, drew the 10 Silent Screen Stars, skillfully capturing each actor's or actress' persona. Hirschfeld's first stamps in 1991 honored American comedians.

Top: The Keystone Cops in one of their many hare-brained chases. The Cops series reached its peak in 1915. Below right: Theda Bara as "Temptress of the Nile." Below: Another Bara seductive pose. She was famed for wearing heavy mascara and sported dresses with low necklines.

Facing page: Keaton planned each scene with care and directed many of his own films. Left: John Gilbert, matinee idol, gained the title of "world's greatest lover," passed down from Valentino. Center: A young Zasu Pitts. She performed in leading and supporting roles in both silent films and the talkies. Right: Harold Lloyd's films often showed him clinging to dangerous ledges or participating in wild chase scenes. He was his own stunt man.

blamed his failure to maintain stardom in "talkies" on a poor voice. Critics said it was no worse than others' and that his studio's choice of roles for him was poor. ZASU PITTS (1898-1963) was a dramatic actress in her silent screen career beginning in 1917, and a scatterbrained comedienne in the "talkies" beginning in 1931. Her greatest performance was in the silent film, *Greed*. She never lacked work and her hand-wringing characters endeared her to audiences. From 1956 to 1959, she acted in the television series, *Oh! Susanna*. HAROLD LLOYD (1893-1971) was one of the most popular comedians of his time, topping Chaplin and Keaton. He began as a hayseed character, then became an optimistic "go-getter," with horn-rimmed glasses, out to conquer the world. His films included chases and slapstick. He received a special Oscar in 1952 for being a master comedian. THE KEYSTONE COPS (1912-1920) were created by film maker Mack Sennett, who made irreverent comedy his specialty. The Cops were described as "men with flailing tailcoats and inverted spittoon helmets, lurching past the camera." Their zany chases included tumbling out of paddy wagons, racing around corners and piling up in confusion. Sennett received a special Oscar in 1937 for his comedies. THEDA BARA (1890-1955), a Cincinnati tailor's daughter, was a 26-year-old extra when a Hollywood publicist transformed her into "a woman of exotic Egyptian parentage" to play a "vamp" who left heartbroken lovers in her wake. Her smoldering eyes expressing passion, she played a bewitching temptress and was an instant hit. Very little of her work survives, although she made 40 films from 1914 to 1919. BUSTER KEATON (1895-1966) was in his parents' vaudeville act at age 3 but left when his father's drinking endangered his safety. As a child, he learned his "deadpan" expression got more laughs than a smile and stoicism became his trademark. His pessimism and acceptance of fate endeared him to audiences. He received an Oscar in 1959.

Place
Stamps
Here

Our transportation needs have fueled invention since the dawn of history. All methods of travel by land, sea and air, have improved dramatically, bringing better, more advanced systems. ✍ The first booklet of stamps depicting early locomotives was issued in 1987. Now come five American type steam locomotives, the most popular locomotives in North America in the 19th Century. Four leading, or "pony" wheels, up front for stability and guidance, and the four tall driving wheels for power characterized the American type. ✍ Railroad history books tell us that in 1835 some 175 steam locomotives were in service in America. By 1840, the 3,328 miles of track equaled the mileage of canals. Between 1860 and 1890, railway mileage grew from 33,000 to 166,000. Steam locomotives, increasingly powerful and efficient, pulled freight, passengers, mail and express cars throughout the nation. William Hudson, Walter McQueen, Wilson Eddy, Theodore Ely and William Buchanan were leading locomotive designers of their day. ✍ William Hudson's GENERAL, built by the Rogers Locomotive Works for the Western and Atlantic Railroad in 1855, became famous for being stolen by northern saboteurs on April 12, 1862, and then retaken by Confederate soldiers. The GENERAL was extensively rebuilt in 1870. ✍ Walter McQueen's JUPITER, built in 1868 by the Schenectady Locomotive Works for the Central Pacific Railroad, met the Union Pacific's NO. 119 at Promontory, Utah, on May 10, 1869, uniting for the first time eastern and western railroads. The golden spike then driven is at Stanford University. ✍ Wilson Eddy's NO. 242 was built in 1874 in the Boston & Albany Railroad's Springfield, Massachusetts, shop. Eddy's designs were called "Eddy Clocks" for smooth-running precision. ✍ Theodore Ely's NO. 10, the Pennsylvania Railroad "Class K" prototype, was built in Altoona in 1881. Her remarkably advanced design made NO. 10 one of the fastest express locomotives in America during the 1880s. ✍ William Buchanan's famous NO. 999, built in 1893 by the New York Central and Hudson River Railroad's West Albany shops, became the first vehicle in the world to exceed 100 miles per hour pulling the Empire State Express in May 1893 near Batavia, New York. ✍

STEAM LOCOMOTIVES

*Top: This popular lithograph called "The Fast Mail" glorified a special mail train in 1874 that sped between New York and Chicago. Note the platform from which a mail sack could be caught as the train passed by. Center: Wilson Eddy's 242 locomotive completed in 1874. Left: The **"Arizona Spike,"** similar to the **"Last Spike"** driven at Promontory, Utah. Facing page: A 19th Century locomotive stops at the wood pile for fuel. Top inset: After the May 10, 1869 ceremony, minor officials posed alongside McQueen's **Jupiter** and the Union Pacific's **NO. 119** at Promontory, Utah.*

Richard Leech, of Orinda, CA, a steam locomotive hobbyist who illustrated the historic series of locomotives issued in 1967, continued his precision work for the five 1994 stamps issued in booklet form. Before his death in 1993, he served clients in North America, Europe and Asia.

CRANES

Top: The North American whooping crane finds a succulent crab for lunch. Bottom: This Ming dynasty (15th-16th Century) silk scroll called "Crane and Pine" is reprinted through courtesy of the Smithsonian Institution's Freer Gallery of Art. Facing page: If ever a species should receive help to survive, this elegant whooping crane and the pair of black-necked cranes (in the inset) deserve a solid effort from humankind.

Zhan Gengxi, born in Haifeng, Hunan Province of the People's Republic of China, is codesigner of the Chinese /U.S. Joint Issue of Cranes. His works reflect traditional and contemporary Chinese techniques, and he bears the title of the State's First Class Painter. His codesigner is Clarence Lee. Clarence Lee also designed the 1993 Year of the Dog stamp.

With their first joint issue of postage stamps, the People's Republic of China and the United States celebrated World Post Day, October 9, 1994, in the capital cities of Beijing and Washington, D.C. The stamps, representing peace and friendship, picture two large and elegant birds native to their respective countries—China's black-necked crane, and the whooping crane, indigenous to North America. ✍ When U.S. postal officials received the proposal to participate in this historic pairing, acceptance was enthusiastic. Discussions about a desirable subject settled upon cranes, for ideals they represent and because both nations seek to protect the endangered species. ✍ Four People's Republic artists and Clarence Lee, a Chinese American graphic artist, submitted concepts to a juried panel. Both sides chose the same finalists, and work commenced to finalize designs. ✍ Cranes existed 60 million years ago, and since earliest man were considered heralds of the gods. Their distinctive calls were believed to remind man of his mortality. ✍ Oriental art has long depicted cranes as creatures of grace and beauty, representing longevity, steadfastness and love. It was customary in olden days to place crane-shaped pins in the coiffures of Chinese women prepared for burial to ensure the departed souls would be accompanied to heaven. ✍ Throughout the world, the cranes' stately courtship dances, in minuet form with formal bows and curtsies, were imitated by natives. American Plains Indians made whistles from cranes' wing bones which they blew going into battle. ✍ Like an airplane take-off, these five-foot-tall birds, with a seven-foot wing-spread, make a running start into the wind but gain altitude more slowly than their mechanical imitators. They also land into the wind, lowering their legs and flapping their wings to gain stability and slow their descent. As many migrant birds, they ride the winds in formation over long distances, often flying a mile above the Earth. ✍ Efforts to increase the species are carefully monitored by the People's Republic of China, Canada and the United States. Vigilance is needed to preserve wetlands and sanctuaries for the cranes' nesting needs and migrating paths. ✍

Place Stamps Here

Place Strip of 5 Stamps Here

Place Strip of 3 Stamps Here

Out of pain, separation from loved ones and tough, physical labor arose jazz, blues, ragtime, gospel and soul music. It was created by slaves who sang songs to the beat of their labors. It was "music sung with a full heart and a troubled spirit." This art has profoundly influenced all American music for more than a century, and these great performers' gifts have enriched the world. ∞ BESSIE SMITH, born into abject poverty in Chattanooga in 1898, is said to have been discovered by Ma Rainey, who asked her to join her tent show. In two years, she achieved success and went to New York to perform in 1923, saying she was "tall and fat and scared to death." In the 1920s she dominated the jazz/blues scene in theatres. Although she was called "the Empress of the Blues," her style of music waned. She died after a car crash in 1937. ∞ BILLIE HOLIDAY (Eleanor Gough McKay) was born in Baltimore, Maryland, in 1915 to a teenage mother and musician father. She moved to New York at age 13 and within a year was singing jazz in Harlem clubs, billed as "Lady Day." She made her recording debut with Benny Goodman in 1933, and as her fame spread she recorded with Teddy Wilson, Count Basie and Artie Shaw. By 1939 she was addicted to alcohol and drugs, her songs were tinged with despair and she was affected by her failed marriages. Her autobiography was made into a movie, *Lady Sings the Blues.* ∞ MILDRED BAILEY (Mildred Rinker) was born in 1907 in Tekoa, Washington. She auditioned for Paul Whiteman and became one of the first female vocalists to sing with a band. She married musician Red Norvo, and in 1936 they started their own band. The first non-Negro to achieve fame singing the blues, she was noted for her clear, bell-like voice, phrasing and excellent diction. She had her own radio show in the mid-forties and won many Esquire awards. She died in 1951. ∞ JIMMY RUSHING, born in Oklahoma City in 1903 of a musical family, had a high-pitched voice that was compelling, warm and penetrating, and he sang both jazz and the blues. He sang in California before joining Count Basie's big band in 1936. He was a headliner with Basie until 1950 when he formed a septet and became even more popular in the U.S. and Europe. He sang with Goodman's band in 1958 and at the Newport Jazz Festival in 1959, performed in

Top: Mildred Bailey made many top selling records between 1937 and 1940. She was always backed by the best jazz musicians on her CBS radio show. Bottom: Jimmy Rushing, the "showman-singer," won the British critics' "Melody Maker" poll in 1957. Facing page: Bessie Smith dominated the jazz/blues scene in the 1920s. She was one of the most successful entertainers of her race in the country.

Howard Koslow (left), of East Norwich, NY, designed 14 stamps before illustrating the Bessie Smith, Billie Holiday, Mildred Bailey and Jimmy Rushing stamps. Julian Allen moved to New York from England in 1973, and his work appears in most major magazines. His first stamp illustrations include Muddy Waters, Robert Johnson, Ma Rainey and Howlin' Wolf.

Top: Ma Rainey in a publicity photograph. Center: Ma with her band about 1925, played to sellout audiences when they played vaudeville theatres in the Midwest. Her unique style brought her stardom. Bottom: Howlin' Wolf made his harmonica "talk" when he wasn't singing. He made a number of successful recordings. Facing page: Billie Holiday's highly individual style is claimed by some as the most potent voice to come out of the jazz traditions. Her ballads reflected the emotions of her personal life. Insets: Muddy Waters' jazz band was the best of its kind in 1951. He was a hit when he toured England in 1958, and he played in a Carnegie Hall folk music concert in 1959.

the film *Funzapoppin* and won a British critics' poll in 1957 as the No. 1 Male Vocalist. ✍ MUDDY WATERS (McKinley Morganfield) was born in Mississippi in 1912. By age 10, he sang and played the harmonica and learned to play a homemade guitar. When his mother died, he moved to his grandmother's home in Clarksdale and worked in the cotton fields. Alan Lomax recorded his music for the Library of Congress. Waters performed in New Orleans, Memphis and Chicago, and his records were played throughout the South. His electric "slide guitar" accompanied his physical vocals that appealed to audiences. He was a hit in Europe before he died in 1983. ✍ ROBERT JOHNSON, born near Clarksdale, Mississippi, around 1911, played the harmonica as a boy and wanted to play the guitar. He hung around joints hoping to learn from musicians. His parents objected, he ran away for about six months, and when he returned he amazed everyone with his guitar playing. He sang the blues, revealing a tormented spirit possibly triggered by his feelings about a defective eye. When an agent looked for him to perform at Carnegie Hall, he learned Robert had been poisoned and died. He was considered one of the most brilliant country blues artists. ✍ MA RAINEY (Gertrude Malissa Nix Pridgett), born in Columbus, Georgia, in 1896, first sang at age 14 at a home talent show. She married Will Rainey from a tent show at 18, and joined the show. The blues became Ma's standard offering. She sang with such power and feeling in her deep contralto voice, she was billed as "The Mother of the Blues." Ma formed a tent show and made several records, some with trumpeter Louis Armstrong. She retired in 1934 and bought two small theatres before her death in Georgia in 1939. ✍ HOWLIN' WOLF (Chester Burnett) was born in 1909 on a plantation in Sunflower County, Mississippi. His career lends proof that his state was a "major birthplace of the blues." His hard, aggressive singing style was influenced by other singers from his part of the country. He worked at a plantation near Memphis, served in the army in World War II and returned to the plantation after his discharge from service. He founded his own band in the 1940s and worked for awhile as a disk jockey in West Memphis, then moved to Chicago where he and Muddy Waters dominated the blues scene in the 1950s. ✍

Muddy Waters

Place
Stamp
Here

Place
Stamp
Here

Holidays are for everyone young and old, of all races religions and nationalities. These stamps help to bring us together. ∽ TRADITIONAL HOLIDAY. A playful infant reaching upward to place a wreath of roses on his adoring mother's head offers a sweet and intimate portrait for the 1994 traditional Holiday stamp. ∽ Created in 1663 by Elisabetta Sirani, the painting is from the Holladay collection given to the National Museum of Women in the Arts in Washington, D.C., by its founder, Wilhelmina Cole Holladay, and her husband, Wallace F. Holladay. ∽ Elisabetta Sirani was born in Bologna, Italy, in 1638, a daughter of a minor artist, Giovanni Andrea Sirani. By age 17 she sold two works, and at 24 had her own studio and school for women painters and earned enough money to support her family. ∽ She died mysteriously in August 1665 at age 27. She was buried near the artist who most influenced her, Guido Reni. In addition to 170 paintings, Sirani produced etchings and numerous drawings, some in the Crown collection at Windsor Castle. A major work, the *Finding of Moses*, is in New York's Metropolitan Museum. The Madonna on this year's stamp is considered the finest she painted on the subject. CONTEMPORARY HOLIDAY. This year's contemporary Holiday stamp pictures a stocking filled with toys and a candy cane, a practice with roots in ancient ceremonies. ∽ For example, Saint Nicholas, born in Turkey around 278 A.D., was revered for kindness and miracles, and traders spread legends of his deeds. By the 12th Century in France, the exchange of gifts in his name began. ∽ Naughty children learned that if they behaved, he would give them sweets and toys; if bad, they got switches. Dutch children put wooden shoes stuffed with hay on the doorsteps for St. Nick's horse to eat on his journey. Today, cookies and milk or a soft drink refresh Santa. St. Nick is today's Santa Claus. ∽ Holiday stocking illustrations repeat the tradition. Thomas Nast, the famed American cartoonist, perpetuated the custom from 1864 to 1886 with his popular version of Santa in *Harper's* magazine. Holiday stockings, both real and customized, are now hung for adults and children, to hold gifts, sweets and even an occasional switch! ∽

Top: Elisabetta Sirani painted this youthful head of Christ. Center: Sirani's undated etching on paper of the Madonna and Child with St. John the Baptist is part of the Holladay Collection in the National Museum of Women in the Arts. Facing page: In this Christmas Eve scene, Santa looks over a young, sleeping child awaiting his visit.

Veteran typographer Bradbury Thompson (left), of Riverside, CT, created the design for the traditional Holiday stamp by Renaissance artist, Elisabetta Sirani. Lou Nolan, of McLean, VA, provided a familiar symbol of the holiday season with a gift-filled stocking. Nolan designed the 1993 pull-toy Holiday stamps.

On February 10, 1994, many people of Chinese descent cheerily greeted each other with the phrase, "Gung-Hey-Fat-Choy" which means "Happy New Year." With colorful parades, fireworks and special feasts in their homes, they celebrated the Chinese Year of the Dog. ∽ The Chinese lunar calendar is determined by the phase of the moon and does not occur on January 1. The Year of the Dog ends January 30, 1995, to be followed by the Year of the Boar on January 31, 1995. The next Year of the Dog begins January 29, 2006, 12 years hence. ∽ When and where did it begin? The studies of astronomy and astrology are said to have originated in the fertile valley between the Tigris and Euphrates Rivers by one of the world's earliest advanced civilizations—the Sumerians. They established a 12-month calendar, and the positions of the constellations throughout the year were said to determine success or failure of significant events and personal fates. The Egyptians, Greeks and Romans adopted this calendar, with variations in names of the months. ∽ The Oriental world, however, had significant differences, the chief being a 12-year lunar calendar cycle instead of a 12-month Gregorian calendar. Legend says that before Buddha left the Earth, he summoned all the animals to announce his intent. First to arrive was the Rat, then the Ox, Tiger, Rabbit, Dragon, Snake, Horse, Sheep, Monkey, Rooster, Dog and Boar. Buddha assigned each a specific year in the order of its arrival. Other complex factors were brought to bear, such as the five main elements of wood, fire, earth, metal and water. The animal year in which you were born was believed to profoundly influence your life. ∽ One born in a Year of the Dog is said to be honest, loyal, intelligent and willing to listen to reason, but tends to be a pessimist. He or she relates best to persons born in the Years of the Horse and Tiger. ∽ Astrology has no official standing in the People's Republic of China, but traditions disappear slowly. Many still celebrate centuries-old practices, and Oriental fortune-tellers still rely upon almanacs and calendars produced yearly in Hong Kong. ∽

Top right: An earthenware dog from the Han Dynasty (206 B.C.-221 A.D.) is part of the Avery Brundage Collection in San Francisco's Asian Art Museum. At left: San Francisco's Chinatown New Year's decorations symbolize good fortune. Facing page: A festival dragon dances in the streets of Seattle's Chinatown. Top inset: A Lion Dance celebrates the Oriental New Year in Oahu, Hawaii. Center inset: A vigorous waist-drum performance in New York. Bottom inset: The Kong Chow Buddhist Temple in San Francisco's Chinatown.

Clarence Lee, of Honolulu, HI, displays versatility as designer of the Year of the Dog stamp and codesigner of the Chinese/U.S. Joint Issue stamps. Lee graduated first in his class at Yale's School of Art and Architecture.

Place Stamp Here

C R E D I T S

Special acknowledgment is given to the following contributors to this publication:

FRONT COVER: © Telegraph Colour Library/FPG International. **TITLE PAGE:** *Underwater scene,* © S. Frink/ALLSTOCK; *Valentino,* Photofest; *Valentino poster,* Courtesy of the Kobal Collection. **CONTENTS:** *The Last Spike,* California State Railroad Museum; *Soccer,* © Tony Stone Images; *Charlie Chaplin,* Academy of Motion Picture Arts and Sciences; *Doves and roses,* © 1994 The Gifted Line, from the John Grossman Collection of Antique Images; *Roses,* © Tim Daniel: PHOTO/NATS. **INTRODUCTION:** *Edward Murrow,* Archive Photos; *Skiing,* © Vandystadt/Allsport; *Refugee women,* National Archives; *Buffalo Soldier,* Culver Pictures; *Buffalo Bill Cody's gun,* Buffalo Bill Historical Center; *Nat King Cole,* Ray Avery Jazz Archives; *Clara Bow,* Kobal Collection; *James Thurber,* James Thurber Literary Properties © 1929, 1951; *Bing Crosby,* Michael Ochs Archives. **NORMAN ROCKWELL:** *Rockwell portrait,* National Portrait Gallery/Smithsonian Institution, Art Resources; *"Saturday Evening Post" covers,* © 1953, 1929 The Norman Rockwell Family Trust; *Rockwell at easel* (both), Bettmann Archives; *Rockwell with model,* FPG International; *Rockwell* (photograph), © Clemens Kalischer/ Norman Rockwell painting reproduced by permission of the Norman Rockwell Family Trust; *Rockwell with artwork,* UPI/Bettmann Archives; *Rockwell* (full), Library of Congress. **GARDEN FLOWERS:** *Yellow rose,* © R. Wells/ALLSTOCK; *Zinnias,* © K. Bumgarner/ALLSTOCK; *Day lily,* © John Lynch: PHOTO/NATS; *Gladioli,* © Deborah Crowell: PHOTO/NATS; *Marigold,* © J. Martin/ALLSTOCK. **EDWARD R. MURROW:** *Murrow at table,* Herbert/Archive Photos; *Murrow at typewriter,* UPI/Bettmann Archives; *Murrow with cigarette at CBS,* Bob Stahman/CBS Photo; *Murrow at microphone,* FPG International; *Murrow and Monroe,* UPI/Bettmann Archives. **WONDERS OF THE SEA:** *Clown fish,* © N. Wu/ALLSTOCK; *Non-stinging jellyfish,* G. Ochocki/Photo Researchers; *Anemone city, reef scenic, Fiji, Queen Angel fish;* © S. Frink/ALLSTOCK; *Sea turtle,* © S. Frink/The Waterhouse; *Dolphins,* Flip Nicklin/Minden Pictures; *Fluted giant clam,* Robinson/Pacific Stock; *Butterflyfish,* © N. Wu/ALLSTOCK; *Hermit crab,* Flip Nicklin/Minden Pictures; *Starfish,* © S. Westmoreland/ALLSTOCK. **BUFFALO SOLDIERS:** *10th Cavalry painting,* National Park Service: Fort Davis National Historic Site; *Troop L-9th Cavalry,* Photo by Imperial Photo Gallery, Courtesy Museum of New Mexico ; *10th Cavalry Escort,* Montana Historical Society; *Ret. Sergeant Major,* © Paul A. Rossi; *10th Cavalry crest,* U.S. Army, © Max Reid. **WINTER OLYMPICS:** *Luge,* © Vandystadt/Allsport; *Hockey goalie,* © FPG International/Mackson; *Men's skiing,* © FPG International/Zimmermann; *Cross country skiing,* Duomo; *Skating,* © Powell/Allsport. **WORLD WAR II-1944:** *Flying Fortresses,* Jeff Ethell Collection; *All other photos,* National Archives. **JAMES THURBER:** *Thurber portrait,* UPI/Bettmann Archives; *Thurber drawing,* © Dean/Archive Photos; *Thurber with friends,* Library of Congress; *Thurber with Zeiss Loupe,* Robert Landry, LIFE Magazine © Time Warner; *Thurber with poodle,* Courtesy of the Thurber House Archives; *Dog,* James Thurber Literary Properties © 1932, 1960. **WORLD CUP SOCCER:** *All photos,* © Tony Stone Images. **POPULAR SINGERS:** *Al Jolson, Ethel Waters, Nat King Cole,* Michael Ochs Archives; *Al Jolson, Bing Crosby, Bing Crosby and Dinah Shore, Nat King Cole,* Ray Avery Jazz Archives; *Ethel Merman* (black and white), Archive Photos; *Ethel Merman* (color), National Portrait Gallery/Smithsonian Institution, Art Resources. **DR. ALLISON DAVIS:** *Davis,* Estate of Allison Davis; *Test cover,* © 1952 Psychological Corporation; *Davis with family,* The Estate of Allison Davis; *Davis with children,* © Allison S. Davis. **MOON LANDING:** *Moon pod and astro,* NASA; *Astronauts,* NASA/National Geographic Magazine; *Buzz Aldrin on moon,* NASA; *Buzz Aldrin with flag,* NASA.

LEGENDS OF THE WEST: *Buffalo Bill, Annie Oakley, Geronimo,* Denver Public Library, Western History Dept.; *Nellie Cashman,* from THE OLD WEST: THE WOMEN, photo by John Zimmerman, © 1978 Time-Life Books Inc., courtesy of Thomas Moffat; *Wyatt pistol,* Joe Rosa; *Pickett spurs,* Jim Naramore; *Moccasins,* Buffalo Bill Historical Center; *Chief Joseph,* National Anthropological Archives/National Museum of Natural History, Smithsonian Institution; *"Sacagawea,"* Oil painting 1904, by E.S. Paxson, University of Montana Museum of Fine Arts; *Bat Masterson, Charles Fremont, William Tilghman,* Culver Pictures, Inc.; *Wyatt Earp,* Western History Collections, University of Oklahoma. **LOVE:** *All photos,* © 1994 The Gifted Line, from the John Grossman Collection of Antique Images. **GEORGE MEANY:** *Meany with cigar,* Library of Congress; *Meany with pickets,* UPI/Bettmann Archives; *Portrait of Meany,* Mastro/Archive Photos; *AFL-CIO,* Bettmann Archives. **SILENT SCREEN STARS:** *Clara Bow, Buster Keaton,* and *John Gilbert,* Academy of Motion Picture Arts and Sciences; *Lon Chaney lobby card and poster,* Courtesy of Chaney Enterprises; *Chaplin poster,* National Portrait Gallery/Smithsonian Institution, Art Resources; *Valentino and Harold Lloyd,* Bettmann Archives; *Chaplin on barrel,* Kobal Collection; *Keystone Cops,* AP/Wide World Photos; *Cleopatra,* Aurichio Collection; *Theda Bara,* Archive Photos; *Zasu Pitts,* Photofest. **LOCOMOTIVES:** *19th Century Locomotive,* Archive Photos; *Joining of lines,* Oakland Museum History Department; *"The Fast Mail,"* Collection of Oliver Jensen; *Eddy's No. 242,* Locomotive Engineering, March 1891; *Spike,* Museum of the City of New York, Gift of Mrs. Arthur Whitney. **CRANES:** *Whooping Crane,* Thomas D. Mangelson/Images of Nature; *"Crane and Pine,"* Freer Gallery of Art, Smithsonian Institution; *Crane in zoo,* © Animals Animals/ Jerry Cooke; *Cranes in winter,* © Li Jianhui/Chinese Photographers Association. **JAZZ/BLUES SINGERS:** *Bessie Smith, Muddy Waters* (bottom) and *Mildred Bailey,* Michael Ochs Archives; *Jimmy Rushing,* © 1994 Herb Snitzer/Michael Ochs Archives; *Ma Rainey, Ma with band, Billie Holiday, Muddy Waters* (top), Driggs/Archive Photos; *Howlin' Wolf,* © 1993 Val Wilmer/Michael Ochs Archives. **HOLIDAY:** *Girl with Santa,* © E. Masterson/ALLSTOCK; *Youthful head of Christ,* Elisabetta Sirani, Museo de Arte de Ponce, Luis A. Ferré Foundation, Inc. Ponce, P.R.; *"Madonna and Child with St. John the Baptist,"* Elisabetta Sirani, The National Museum of Women in the Arts, Gift of Wallace and Wilhelmina Holladay. **HAPPY NEW YEAR:** *Chinatown,* © Schermeister/Allstock; *Earthenware dog,* Asian Art Museum of San Francisco, The Avery Brundage Collection; *Festival dragon,* © R. Wells/ALLSTOCK; *Lion dance,* Carini/Pacific Stock; *Waist drum performance,* © Li Jianhui/Chinese Photographers Association; *Buddhist temple,* © P. Schermeister/ALLSTOCK. **CREDITS:** *Charlie Chaplin,* Kobal Collection *Roses,* © R. Stangler/ALLSTOCK.

Special thanks are extended to the following individuals for their contribution to the production of this book: **JEANNE O'NEILL,** narrative text, editing and research. **TERRENCE MCCAFFREY,** creative direction and print quality production. **ROBERTA WOJTKOWSKI,** design, layout, photo editing, and art production. **PHOTOASSIST, INC.,** photo research. **EEI,** editing. **PAUL OVCHINNIKOFF,** print production procurement and supervision.

Top: Sir Charles Chaplin was knighted by Queen Elizabeth II.
Bottom: "Oh, my luve is like a red, red rose
That's newly sprung in June". —Robert Burns